MORPHOGENESIS OF THE BOARD OF DIRECTORS
The independent director as a moral discourse in times of crisis: Case Bankia, Abengoa, Popular and DIA

Finalist of the II Award for Research in Business Ethics - ICADE Banquinter Consumer Finance

AUTHOR

Osvaldo Jorge Castillo
Doctorate in Business Administration
Pontificia Universidad Católica Argentina

July 2019

Castillo, Osvaldo Jorge

MORPHOGENESIS OF THE BOARD OF DIRECTORS

The independent director as a moral discourse in times of crisis: Case Bankia, Abengoa, Popular and DIA/ Osvaldo Jorge Castillo. – Buenos Aires: Castillo, Osvaldo Jorge, 2019.

77 p.; 22 x 15 cm.

ISBN: 9781079941623
Imprint: Independently published

© Dr. Osvaldo Jorge Castillo, 2019

Contact author: prof.ojc@gmail.com

Index

SUMMARY 7
1.1 JUSTIFICATION 9
1.2 INVESTIGATION QUESTIONS 10
2.1 OBJECTIVES 13
   2.1.1 General 13
   2.1.2 Specific 14
2.2 HYPOTHESIS 14
2.3 THEORETICAL FRAMEWORK 14
   2.3.1 The ethical representation of the minority in the council. 14
   2.3.2 Dilemma between speech and action 15
   2.3.3 Types of counselors 19
   2.3.4 Model: theoretical ethical categories of representation 20
   2.3.5 The morphogenesis that preceded exits from ibex-35 .. 22
   2.3.5.1 It is found in C1 and goes abruptly to C2. 23
   2.3.5.2 It is found in C3 and passes briskly to C2. 23
   2.3.5.3 It is found at C3 and abruptly goes to C4. 24
   2.3.5.4 It is found at C4 and passes briskly to C2. 25
3 METHODOLOGY & DEVELOPING 27
   3.1 Structure of the investigation 27
   3.1.2 Type of explanatory investigation 27
   3.1.3 Quantitative investigation 28
   3.1.4 Not experimental 28

3.1.5 Longitudinal panel design 28
3.1.6 Objectives, sub-objectives and hypothesis of the investigation 29
3.2 DEVELOPING 31
3.2.1 Sub-objective 1 31
3.2.1.4 Movements in the IBEX-35 base year 2015 32
3.2.1.5 Movements in the IBEX-35 before the base year 33
3.2.1.6 Movements in the IBEX-35 after the base year 34
3.2.2 Sub-objective 2 36
3.2.2.1 Frequency tables year by year 2013 to 2017 36
3.2.2.2 Total Frequency Table 39
3.3.3 Sub-objective 3 40
3.3.3.1 The exit of the IBEX-35 from the ethical category 40
3.3.4 Specific objective "A" 41
3.3.4.1 Joint likelihood of belonging to a Category and leaving the IBEX-35 41
3.3.4.2 Conditional probability of exit belonging to a category 44
3.3.5 Specific objective "B". 47
3.3.5.1 Analysis of automatic detection of interactions (AID) 47
3.3.5.2 Interpretation 49
3.3.6 Specific objective "C" 51
3.3.6.1 Average loss in quotation when leaving the IBEX-35 51
3.3.6.2 Analysis of automatic detection of interactions (AID) 52
3.3.6.3 Interpretation 53
3.3.7 Overall objective. 55

3.3.7.1	CASE ANALYSIS	55
3.3.7.1.1	BANKIA	55
3.3.7.1.2	ABENGOA	57
3.3.7.1.3	POPULAR	59
3.3.7.1.4	INTERNATIONAL FOOD DISTRIBUTION - DIA	60
4	CONCLUSIONS AND PROPOSAL	63
4.1	CONCLUSIONS	63
4.2	PROPOSAL	65
BIBLIOGRAPHY		67
ANNEXED		69

SUMMARY

Adaptive movements in the microstructure of the board of directors are the center of morphogenesis - a strategy that implements every living organism to stay alive in the future -. In the company, morphogenesis responds to complex systems of interest with privileged information, routed to the implementation strategies that will have probable future consequences. In recent years we have seen deep crises preceded exits of the IBEX-35. Among the most sadly famous we can remember Bankia (2012), Abengoa (2015), Popular (2017) and more recently DIA (2018). The interesting thing is that exits of the IBEX-35 they had something in common: they were preceded by exaggerated variations in the percentages of independent representation concerning floating capital. This curious phenomenon, which we call "morphological abnormality" can be interpreted in different ways: one speech tacit, intended for shareholders and stakeholders, charged with strong moral expectations to transmit confidence; find presumed scapegoats to whom it is to attribute failure; a board of directors acting as a notary or also called a " signature "; a strategy to solve the crisis with highly qualified professionals; or a combination of all of it. Therefore, the study of adaptations of the microstructure of the board of administration turns out to be an innovative approach that can contribute to the development of ethics in the board.

KEYWORDS: BOARD OF DIRECTORS, IBEX-35[1], MORPHOGENESIS, INDEPENDENT DIRECTOR

---

[1] The IBEX 35 is the official index of the Spanish Continuous Exchange. The index is comprised of the 35 most liquid stocks traded on the Continuous market. It is calculated, supervised and published by the Sociedad de Bolsas. The equities use free float shares in the index calculation. The index was created with a base level of 3000 as of December 29, 1989.

Chapter 1

JUSTIFICATION & INVESTIGATION QUESTIONS

1.1 JUSTIFICATION

Much of the scientific management literature points out the importance of the structure of the board of directors in the anticipation of agency problems. They also point out the different ways in which these problems can be minimized, such as : incentives to administrators, division of the functions of first executive or CEO with those of the chairman of the board of directors, proportionality of the representation in the floating capital board and of the hardcore, etc. But no investigation deepens in morphogenesis or dynamic structural changes happening in the board of directors. These changes anticipate, in many cases disastrous consequences event for the interests of minority shareholders.

The first contribution of this work consists of the empirical demonstration of the relationship between the increase in the representation of independent directors on the board of directors with the floating capital and the probable exit of the IBEX-35. The second contribution is the development and application of the model in question, to the IBEX-35 companies that experienced the most important outflows - in terms of economic losses - for minority shareholders in recent years. This investigation is relevant because:

i. Provides a new analysis tool
ii. It allows to understand in-depth the processes prior to the exits of the IBEX-35
iii. Helps to understand how atypical movements affect the representation of the independent director
iv. Explain causal relationships between representation and probability of leaving the IBEX-35

1.2   INVESTIGATION QUESTIONS

Studies carried out confirm the existence of positive results associated with the announcement of appointment or increase in the number of independent directors. This reaction, on the part of the investors, is understandable insofar as the markets are willing to trust this type of adviser. But it also warns of the risks of the possibility that independent directors may not be truly independent of those seeking their appointment (Olivencia, 1999, page 20). Based on this, and taking into account the time elapsed since the publication of the Olivencia Code and the advances in the topic of Corporate Governance, some doubts arise about whether these concepts are still valid:

1. It is child to suspect that a deep crisis looming when the micro-structure of the board inexplicably fits an excessive proportion of independent directors? St would be logical to think that this is an on performance or facade?

2. Are the big scandals for frauds more likely in some configuration of independent directors than in another, and if so, in which?

3. Is there a structural configuration advice - property, more likely to leave the IBEX-35? And if so What?

4. If the above points are confirmed, can events reasonably be predicted that represent potential risks for the minority?

5. If confirmed, could the study of the morphogenesis of the board of directors contribute to the development of ethics and the Code of Good Governance of Listed Companies?

Chapter 2

OBJECTIVES, HYPOTHESIS & THEORETICAL FRAMEWORK

2.1 OBJECTIVES

2.1.1 General

Determine if a specific morphogenesis of the board of directors preceded the deep crises that most affected the minority shareholders in the companies that left the IBEX-35.

2.1.2 Specific

A) Determine if there is a morphological configuration more likely to exit the IBEX-35, and if so, what it is.

B) Estimate the configuration contribution morphological to the probability of leaving the IBEX-35.

C) Determine an average loss value per probable exit of the IBEX-35 for such probable configuration.

2.2 HYPOTHESIS

The exits of the IBEX-35 due to deep crises were preceded by an atypical change in the proportion of independent directors, above proportional representation usual floating capital.

2.3 THEORETICAL FRAMEWORK

2.3.1 The ethical representation of the minority in the council

Floating capital is the part of the share capital that is held by small investors or minority shareholders. To prevent, as far as possible, privileges and irresponsibilities on the part of the members of the Boards of Directors that harm these shareholders, the ' The Cadbury Report ' (Cadbury, 1992) in the United Kingdom, making the implementation of more rigorous aspects of financial supervision of companies. With the same fundamental purpose of protecting minority shareholders in the US, the ' Sarbanes-Oxley Law ' (Sarbanes & Oxley, 2002) . For its part in Spain, the Good Governance Code of the Listed Companies of the CNMV (CNMV, 2015) of February 2015 includes a series of good corporate governance practices, whose purpose is that these companies are managed in an appropriate manner and transparent as an essential factor for generating value in companies. It should be noted that the use of this Code is voluntary along with the principle of "comply or explain", this means that, in case of non-compliance, the reason must be explained, being the system followed both in the main countries of the European Union as in other developed countries. This Code is thus an excellent reference for good corporate governance practices.

Article 11 of said Code establishes the composition of the board of directors, in this regard it says: "The board of directors shall have a balanced composition, with a large majority of non-executive directors and an appropriate proportion between proprietary and independent directors, representing the latter, in general, at least half of the directors.

As can be seen, the composition of the Board of Directors is extremely important since the representation of the different interests at the highest level within society depends on it. It is logical to think then that, sometimes under different circumstances, changes in the structure of the Board -Director- are reflecting changes in direction, policy, or interests in the company that will have a future impact on the different stakeholders.

2.3.2 Dilemma between speech and action

Frederick Bird and James Waters expose their concern about what they call the marked silence that managers and executives exhibit with respect to ethical behavior in business (Bird & Waters, 1989). Moreover, the authors emphasize that silence is maintained in the same dimension also in those cases in which it acts respecting a scale of ethical values in the business world.

When it comes to appealing to the motives of this behavior of businessmen, it is argued that managers simply take for granted the scarce relationship between ethics and business, which is reaffirmed when some illegal activities are labeled as unethical.

On the basis of this hypothesis, the authors establish a series of relationships between action, discourse and ethical and moral norms in the behavior of managers. In his opinion it is possible to conceive four types of models of relations between the mentioned elements: the first model is identified with that scenario in which the discourse and the action coincide and correspond to the moral expectations. The authors call the "congruent moral behavior model." The second congruence model is represented by that situation in which coherence between discourse and action is manifested, but none of them is guided by moral expectations. Called "congruent model of immoral or amoral conduct".

Likewise, they define two models in which the incongruence between discourse and action prevails. In the first one, a different discourse towards moral standards is shown that is not reflected precisely in the behavior of the actors. It is the "model of hypocrisy or moral weakness" synthesized in the discrepancy between action and message. Finally, the scenario of silence or moral silence is what arouses the preferential attention of the authors. This model shows a reality of mutism in the communication of morals and ethics by managers, but they are expected to act according to moral standards.

RELATIONSHIP BETWEEN DISCOURSE AND MORAL ACTION		
ACTIONS / **SPEECH**	Actions followed by Morales expectations	Actions NOT followed by Morales expectations
Moral terms used in the speech	Congruent moral behavior model	Facade model (discrepancy between action and message)
Moral terms Not used in the speech	Model of silence or moral mutism (avoid talking about morality)	Congruent model of amoral conduct (coherence between speech and action)

The authors investigate the causes of this phenomenon, in which they tend to avoid talking about morals since this can represent a threat to harmony, and to the image of power and effectiveness. For its part, the consequences of moral silence can lead to moral amnesia, a narrow concept of morality, moral stress for managers, negligence for moral abuse and lowering of moral standards.

Applying the Bird and Waters model to the moral model that the company would probably apply to the minority investor, to itself, for example:

> • A company with a proportion of independent directors that greatly exceeds the proportion of free float transmits an idea or message of tranquility and support to the minority investor. We will say that this company uses a clear moral discourse towards their interests, giving them direct or indirect support and guarantees. If the actions of said company coincide with the expectations thus

communicated in his speech, then we say that the company in question has a model of congruent moral conduct. If, on the other hand, the shares are not followed by moral expectations, such as a significant issue in times of recession that dilutes the value of the shares of the former shareholders, then we are in the presence of a model of hypocrisy or façade since, his speech, intrinsically in favor does not coincide with his actions against minority interests.

- A company that has a representation below the proportion of floating capital, clearly does not have a moral discourse towards the minority, that is, does not create false expectations, but , if it exercises actions followed by moral expectation, such as a high profit per share with high dividends, then it applies a model of moral mutism, that is, its board of directors does not say tacitly : "I worry about the minority", but nevertheless it worries about them in the facts.

2.3.3 Types of counselors

The types of directors in Spanish companies are:

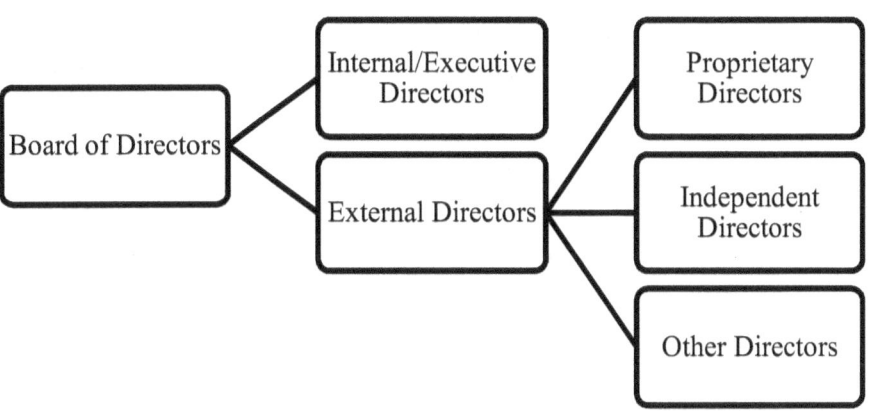

Typology of directors in Spanish companies Source **(Stein & Plaza, 2011)**

- **Internal / executive directors:** They are members of the management team of the company, who occupy a position on the Board of Directors. They could have double executive - shareholder status, although it is not necessary. Normally they have a technical profile related to their management work (financial, industrial, commercial, among others)

- **External Directors:** One of the most difficult tasks of the external counselor is to decide if the administration is doing a good job (Mace, 1975, page 17).

o   **Proprietary directors**: Directors representing a percentage of the company's shares. They are people unrelated to the daily management of the company, but have a direct link with it and the shareholder or group of controlling shareholders (significant shareholders). In family businesses they usually represent those family branches that are not directly related to management. Also, they could sometimes represent shareholders who delegate the representation of their participation.

o   **Independent directors**: They are appointed in response to their personal and professional conditions, who can perform their duties without being conditioned by relations with the company, its significant shareholders or its directors. They provide an external, professional and independent vision with the aim of generating value for shareholders. They are called to represent floating capital and hence its importance to minority shareholders.

o   **Other directors:** Those who cannot be considered as proprietary or independent. The presence of this type of counselor in the Board is justified given their experience and knowledge. For example, an executive could be classified as *another director* who, due to retirement, ceases to perform his management duties (Stein & Plaza, 2011, page 3) .

2.3.4   Model: theoretical ethical categories of representation

Following the recommendations of the Code of Good Governance, the "council - property" matrix was designed. In this matrix, the rows show the percentage of minority representation in the board of directors-grouped from 0% to 50% in the bottom row and, greater than 50% to 100% in the top row. The columns show the free float-grouped from 0% to 50% in the first and, greater than 50% to 100% of free float in the second. This division makes it possible to quickly visualize how the principle of proportionality is fulfilled, notwithstanding that the CNMV recommendation itself clarifies that this principle is not an exact mathematical rule but that it attempts to ensure that independent directors have sufficient weight on the board of directors (CNMV, 2015, page 27). The microstructure of the board of directors will be analyzed with the Matrix "Board of Directors - Property", from which the "theoretical ethical categories of representation" will be obtained. The following illustration shows the proposed "Board of Directors - Property" matrix and the four resulting ethical representation categories:

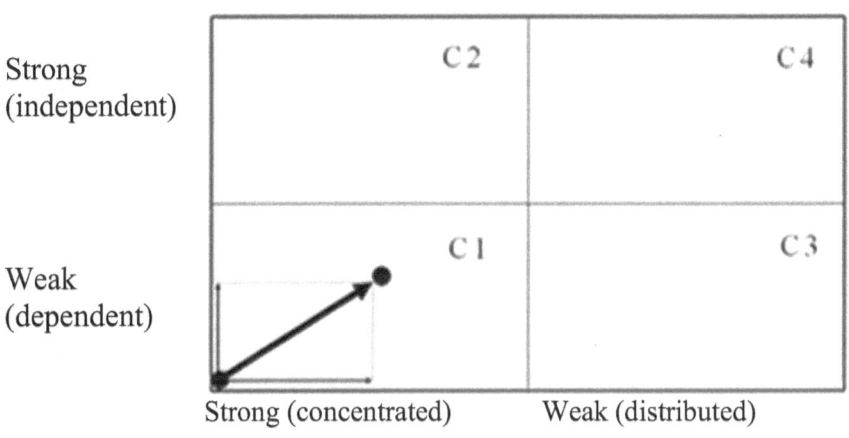

Matrix Board of Directors - Property
Source: Own elaboration.

The companies, throughout their lives for various reasons, modify the structure of their property. In order to avoid the probable problems of agency, these changes should be reflected in adaptations of the structure of its Board of Directors, what we have called its "morphogenesis". Studying morphogenesis as the result of the variables "structure of ownership " and "structure of the Board" is revealing, given the importance of the independent director in the Code of Good Governance.

For third parties, the morphogenesis of the board of directors is the discourse that the company uses. The strategies, embodied in concrete actions, will demonstrate over time the true purpose of morphogenesis. Discourse, therefore, precedes actions. Thus, if the expectations generated by the discourse are met with the actions, then the moral or immorality will be congruent. On the other hand, if actions do not comply with the expectations emanating from the discourse, there is hypocrisy or deceit, which denotes facade morphogenesis.

We can imagine different combinations of ownership and representation, for example, when a company starts - entrepreneurship-, it does not have a board of directors and its property is concentrated in its founding partner, so it will have a strong property - a single partner takes all the decisions-, with weak or nonexistent advice (not there who controls it). As the company grows, if it needs to increase capital and it is quoted on the stock exchange, the number of shareholders without direct representation on the board of directors may also grow, thus losing power. This loss of power should be counteracted by an increasing number of independent directors on the board of directors representing them. Morphogenesis can vary according to the case, resulting in movements in the "advice - property" matrix. In this paper, we will analyze the movements in the matrix that preceded deep crises that ended in exits of the IBEX-35.

2.3.5 The morphogenesis that preceded exits from ibex-35

As we said, the "morphological anomaly" that preceded the most shocking crises in recent years, had in common exaggerated variations in the percentages of independent representation

concerning floating capital -more independent directors than usual in its board of directors-.
Analyzing the cases, we can differentiate four types of changes of direction in the representation, which mean atypical modifications of the proportion of independent directors concerning the floating capital.

2.3.5.1 It is found in C1 and goes abruptly to C2.

The proportion of independent directors increased sharply. This expansion could, at first sight, signify a strengthening of the representativeness of the interest for the floating capital in the company or simply to improve the image before the investors.

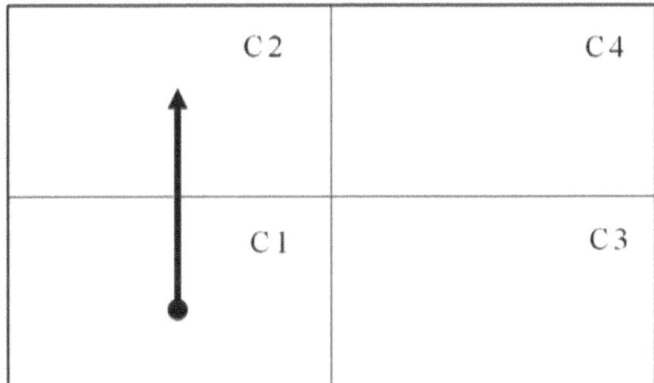

An abrupt change from C1 to C2.
Source: Own elaboration.

2.3.5.2 It is found in C3 and passes briskly to C2.

A company with a dispersed capital and a minority of independent directors increases its representation on the board of directors above 50%, and its floating capital decreases below 50%.

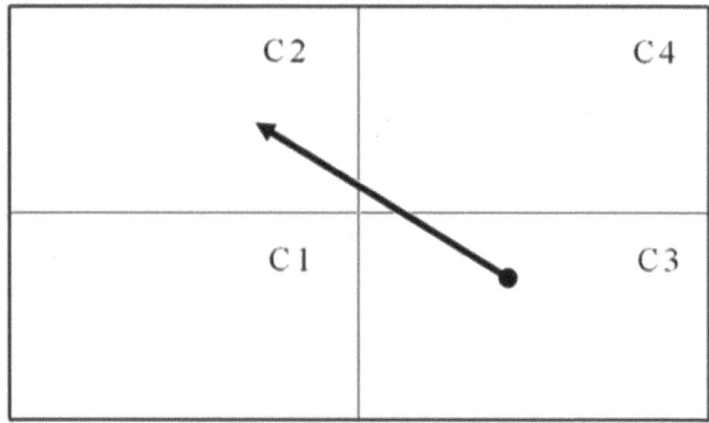

An abrupt change from C3 to C2

2.3.5.3 It is found at C3 and abruptly goes to C4.

The proportion of independent directors is increased. This extension may mean a strengthening of the representativeness of the interest for the floating capital in the company or a simple improvement of its image before the investors or an effort to improve the performance in general.

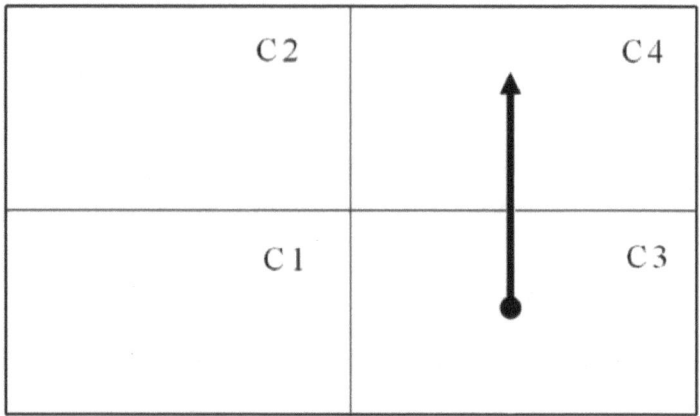

An abrupt change from C3 to C4
Source: Own elaboration.

2.3.5.4 It is found at C4 and passes briskly to C2.

When the company becomes controlled or when it repurchases its shares radically modifying its capital structure, maintaining the structure of its Board of Directors.

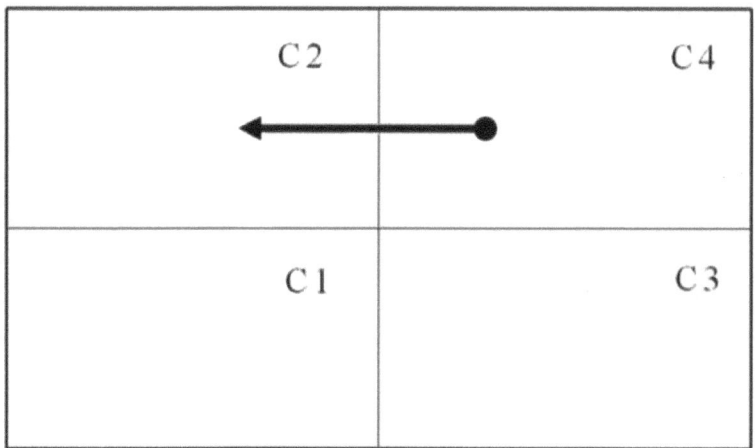

An abrupt change from C4 to C2.
Source: Own elaboration.

Chapter 3

3 METHODOLOGY & DEVELOPING

3.1 Structure of the investigation

From the analysis of the scientific literature and other research related to the issue of independent directors, it is concluded that this research is relevant since, if the hypothesis is verified, it will be very useful for investors, minority shareholders, and academics. The main usefulness of this research is the explanation of the causal relationships between abrupt changes in the theoretical ethical category and the probability of leaving the IBEX-35.

3.1.2 Type of explanatory investigation

Given that the interest is focused on explaining in what cases the phenomenon of a greater probability of leaving the IBEX-35 occurs, the investigation is explanatory (Sampieri Hernández, Fernández Collado, & Lucio Baptista, Research Methodology (First edition), 1991, page 98). In the research, causal relationships between the variables under study are described.

3.1.3 Quantitative investigation

The investigation will be quantitative, of evaluation and interpretation of the procedures and data in connection with the theoretical framework (López Alonso, 2006, page 30).

3.1.4 Not experimental

The research is not experimental since it was done without deliberately manipulating variables, what will be done is, therefore, to observe the phenomena as they occur in their natural context and then analyze them (Sampieri Hernández, Fernández Collado, & Lucio Baptista, Methodology of research (First edition), 1991, page 189).

3.1.5 Longitudinal panel design

This design collects data on the variables in two or more moments, to evaluate the change in them (Sampieri Hernández, Fernández Collado, & Lucio Baptista, Research Methodology (First edition), 1991, page 201). The same IBEX-35 companies with headquarters in Spain will be selected, from 2013 to 2018, taking into account the exits and entries to calculate the exit probabilities of the IBEX-35.

3.1.6 Objectives, sub-objectives and hypothesis of the investigation

ELEMENTS OF THE PROPOSED MODEL		OBJECTIVES, SUB-OBJECTIVES AND HYPOTHESES OF THE INVESTIGATION
1	CATEGORIZING COMPANIES ACCORDING TO THE MODEL: THEORETICAL ETHICAL REPRESENTATION CATEGORIES	**Sub-objective 1.** Classify all movements of entries and exits of the IBEX-35, by the ethical category of theoretical representation.
		Sub-objective 2. Set up a table of total frequencies 2013 - 2017 with the categories, entries, and exits of the IBEX-35.
		Sub-objective 3. Calculate the conditional probability of exit the IBEX-35 from to a theoretical ethical category.
2	MEASURE THE IMPORTANCE OF THE VARIABLE: THEORETICAL ETHICAL CATEGORY OF REPRESENTATION AT THE EXIT OF THE IBEX-35	**Specific objective "A".** Determine if there is a THEORETICAL ETHICAL CATEGORY (morphological configuration) more likely to exit the IBEX-35 and if so, which one is it.
		Specific objective "B". Estimate the

	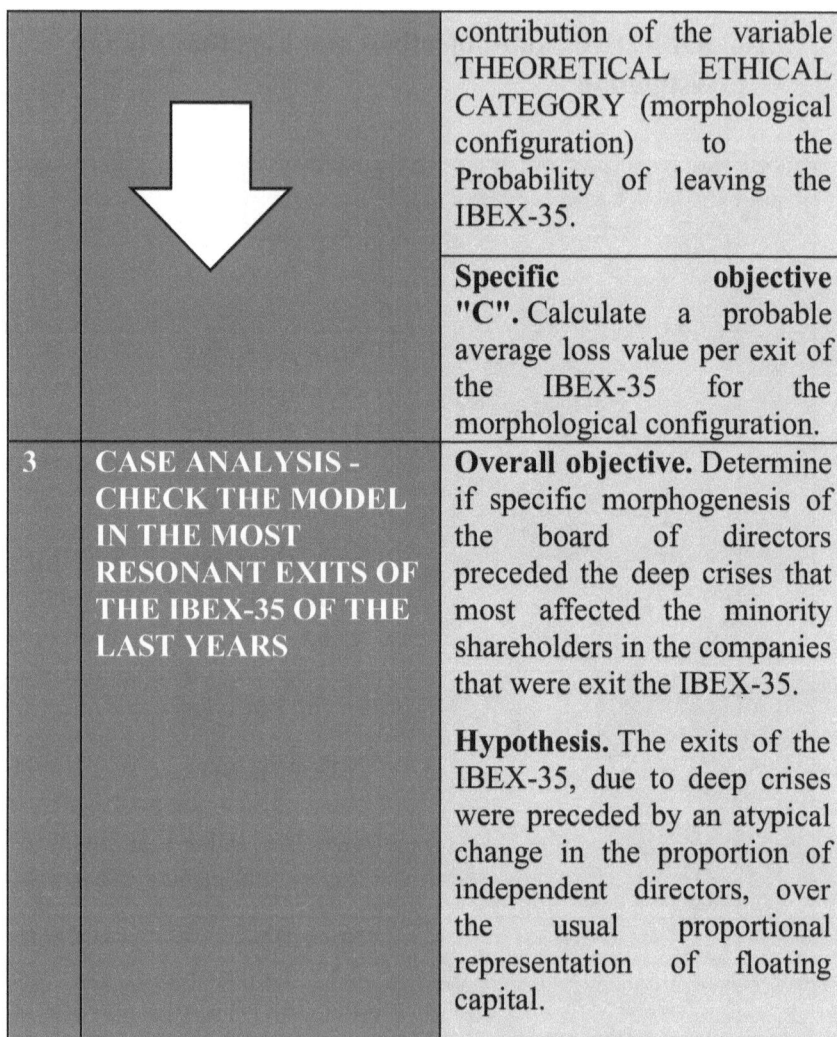	contribution of the variable THEORETICAL ETHICAL CATEGORY (morphological configuration) to the Probability of leaving the IBEX-35.
		Specific objective "C". Calculate a probable average loss value per exit of the IBEX-35 for the morphological configuration.
3	**CASE ANALYSIS - CHECK THE MODEL IN THE MOST RESONANT EXITS OF THE IBEX-35 OF THE LAST YEARS**	**Overall objective.** Determine if specific morphogenesis of the board of directors preceded the deep crises that most affected the minority shareholders in the companies that were exit the IBEX-35.
		Hypothesis. The exits of the IBEX-35, due to deep crises were preceded by an atypical change in the proportion of independent directors, over the usual proportional representation of floating capital.

3.2 DEVELOPING

3.2.1 Sub-objective 1

> Classify all movements of entries and exits of the IBEX-35, by the ethical category of theoretical representation.

3.2.1.1 Technique used: Empirical probability

For the calculation of the probability, we will base in what we have called "the method of the analysis of the morphogenesis of the microstructure of the board of administration". They will be counted in a frequency table, per year, and by "theoretical ethical categories", all exits, and entrances in the Spanish stock index. OPA is not will be taken for the calculation of probabilities of exits for a crisis.

3.2.1.2 Population subject of study IBEX-35 base year 2015

To carry out this analysis, it will be taken as the base year 2015. All entries and exits will be recorded, according to the theoretical ethics category and the date on which the novelty in the conformation of the IBEX-35 occurred. The movements before the base year will be monitored from 2013, and after the formation of the IBEX-35 to 2017 (The IAGC 2018 were not presented at the time of this work).

3.2.1.3 Secondary source

- Historical composition of the IBEX-35 published by the Madrid Stock Exchange[2].
- Annual Corporate Governance Report, National Securities Market Commission (www.cnmv.es)

---

[2] http://www.bolsamadrid.es/docs/SBolsas/InformesSB/compoIBEX.pdf

- Value of the shares before the exits of the IBEX-35 Google finance (www.google.com/finance).

3.2.1.4 Movements in the IBEX-35 base year 2015

IBEX-35 to December 2015[3]				
Company		**Category**	**Movement**	**Date**
Abengoa	ABG	3	Exit	27/11/2015
Abertis	ABE	3		
Acciona	ANA	2	Exit /Enter	22/6-20/7/2015
Acerinox	ACX	3	Exit	22/06/2015
ACS	ACS	3		
Aena	AENA	1	Enter	22/06/2015
Amadeus	AMA	5		
Bankia	BKIA	2		
Bankinter	BKT	3		
BBVA	BBVA	5		
BME	BME	3	Exit	22/06/2015
Caixabank	CABK	1		
Día	DIA	5		
Enagas	ENG	5		
Endesa	ELE	1		
FCC	FCC	1		
Ferrovial	FER	3		
Gamesa	GAM	4		
Gas Natural	GAS	1		
Grifols	GRF	5		
IAG	IAG	5		

[3] Acerlomittal Because it has its headquarters in Luxembourg City, it is not considered in the analysis

Iberdrola	IBE	5		
Inditex	ITX	1		
Indra	IDR	4		
Jazztel	JAZ	4	Exit x OPA[4]	24/06/2015
Mapfre	MAP	1		
Mediaset	TL5	1		
Merlin Prop	MRL	4	Enter	21/12/2015
OHL	OHL	1		
Popular	POP	3		
REE	REE	5		
Repsol	REP	3		
Sabadell	SAB	4		
Sacyr	SCYR	3		
Santander	SAN	4		
Técnicas Reunidas	TRE	5		
Telefónica	TEF	3		

3.2.1.5 Movements in the IBEX-35 before the base year

Movements before the base year 2015, for the periods 2013 and 2014, and their impact on the respective contributions.

IBEX-35 to December 2013				
Company		Category	Movement	Date
Viscofan	VIS	3	Enter	02/01/2013

---

[4] The exit of Jazztel by OPA does not count as an output for performance

Jazztel	JAZ	4	Enter	23/04/2013
Ebro Foods	EBRO	1	Enter	01/07/2013
Sacyr	SCYR	3	Enter	01/10/2013
Bankia	BKIA	2	Enter	23/12/2013
Gamesa	GAM	4	Enter	23/12/2013
Bankia	BKIA	2	Exit	02/01/2013
Gamesa	GAM	4	Exit	02/01/2013
Abengoa	ABG	3	Exit	01/07/2013
ACX	ACX	3	Exit	23/12/2013
Endesa	ELE	1	Exit	23/12/2013

IBEX-35 to december 2014				
Company		Category	Movement	Date
Abengoa	ABG	1	Enter	23/06/2014
Endesa	ELE	1	Enter	22/12/2014
Ebro Foods	EBRO	1	Exit	23/06/2014
Viscofan	VIS	4	Exit	22/12/2014

3.2.1.6 Movements in the IBEX-35 after the base year

IBEX-35 to december 2016				
Company		Category	Movement	Date
Celnext - Telecom	CLNX	1	Enter	21/06/2016
Viscofan	VIS	3	Enter	21/06/2016
FCC	FCC	1	Exit x OPA[5]	18/07/2016
Meliá	MEL	1	Enter	08/08/2016
OHL	OHL	1	Exit	21/06/2016
Sacyr	SCYR	3	Exit	21/06/2016

---

[5] The exit of FCC by OPA does not count as output for performance

IBEX-35 to december 2017				
Company		Category	Movement	Date
Colonial	COL	3	Enter	08/06/2017
Popular	POP	3	Exit	07/06/2017

3.2.2 Sub-objective 2.

Set up a table of total frequencies 2013 - 2017 with the categories, entries, and exits of the IBEX-35.

3.2.2.1 Frequency tables year by year 2013 to 2017

IBEX COMPOSITION AT 12-DECEMBER 2012[6]			
Abengoa	Bme	Iberdrola	Sabadell
Abertis	Caixabank	Inditex	Sacyr
Acciona	Dia	Indra	Santander
Acerinox	Enagas	Intl cons airlin	Tecnicas reu
Acs	Endesa	Mapfre	Telefónica
Amadeus	Fcc	Mediaset	
Arcelormittal	Ferrovial	Ohl	
Bankia	Gamesa	Popular	
Bankinter	Gas natural	Red electrica	
Bbva	Grifols	Repsol	

---

[6] Renta4 https://www.r4.com/analisis/informes/ibex_20121205.pdf

2013 Frequencies					
Category	2012	Enter	Exit	Exit x opa	Remain
C1	8	1	1		8
C2	2	1	1		2
C3	11	1	2		10
C4	4	2	1		5
C5	9				9
	34	5	5		34

2014 Frequencies					
Category	2013	Enter	Exit	Exit x opa	Remain
C1	8	2	1		9
C2	2				2
C3	10				10
C4	5		1		4
C5	9				9
	34	2	2		34

2015 Frequencies					
Category	2014	Enter	Exit	Exit x opa	Remain
C1	9	1			10
C2	2	1	1		2
C3	10	1	2		9
C4	4	1	0	1	4
C5	9				9
	34	4	3	1	34

Note: Jazztel starts from C4; this frequency is not output due to crisis.

2016 Frequencies					
Category	2015	Enter	Exit	Exit x opa	Remain
C1	10	2	1	1	10
C2	2				2
C3	9	1	1		9
C4	4				4
C5	9				9
	34	3	2	1	34

Note: FCC leaves from C1; this frequency is not exit due to crisis.

2017 Frequencies					
Category	2016	Enter	Exit	Exit x opa	Remain
C1	10	1		1	10
C2	2				2
C3	9	1	1		9
C4	4				4
C5	9				9
	34	2	1	1	34

Note: Gamesa goes out and Siemens
Gamesa Renewable enters Energy from C1, this frequency is not exit by crisis.

3.2.2.2 Total Frequency Table

2013-2017 Frequencies					
Category	Before	Enter	Exit	Exit x opa	Remain
C1	45	7	3	2	47
C2	10	2	2		10
C3	49	4	6		47
C4	21	3	2	1	21
C5	45	0	0		45
	170	16	14	3	170

Note: Total frequency of 170 observations divided by the 5 periods studied (2013-2014-2015-2016-2017) results in 34 companies analyzed since, as clarified, Acerlor Mittal is not part of this study because it has its parent company in Luxembourg.

3.3.3 Sub-objective 3

> Calculate the conditional probability of exit the IBEX-35 from to a theoretical ethical category.

3.3.3.1 The exit of the IBEX-35 from the ethical category

Next, the exits of the IBEX-35 are detailed by the theoretical ethical category of the "council- property" matrix:

COMP.	MATRIX					YEAR
	C1	C2	C3	C4	C5	
GAM				X		2013
BKIA		X				2013
ABG			X			2013
ACX			X			2013
ELE	X					2013
EBRO	X					2014
VIS				X		2014
ANA		X				2015
BME			X			2015
ABG			X			2015
OHL	X					2016
SCYR			X			2016
POP			X			2017
TOTAL	3	2	6	2	0	

Source: self-made

3.3.4 Specific objective "A"

> Determine if there is a THEORETICAL ETHICAL CATEGORY (morphological configuration) more likely to exit the IBEX-35 and if so, which one is it.

3.3.4.1 Joint likelihood of belonging to a Category and leaving the IBEX-35

The joint probability is the probability that several events are simultaneously fulfilled, in statistics it is written as P (A ∩ B), in our case, that a company belongs to a given category and that it leaves the IBEX-35. The Venn diagram clearly illustrates this concept for the intersection of the "Ci" CATEGORIES with "IBEX-35 Exits". The fact that the ellipses overlap indicates that some points of the sample are contained both in "Ci" and in the set of "Outputs of the IBEX-35". The area where the ellipses overlap is the intersection: it contains the points of the sample that are in both "Ci" and "Exit of the IBEX-35".

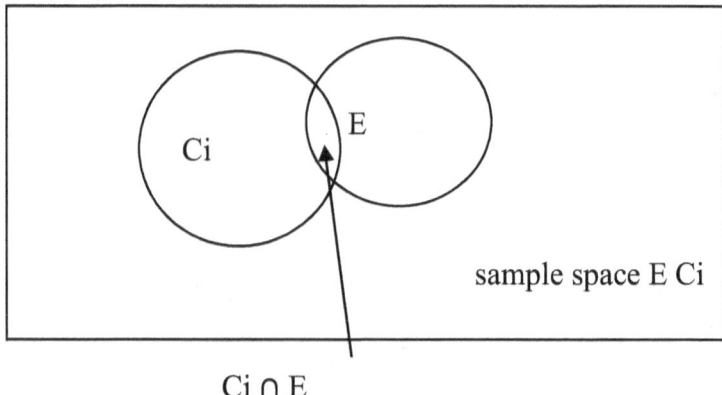

$Ci \cap E$

The following table shows the respective joint probabilities for all the Categories of the Council-Property Matrix from 2013 to 2017.

2013-2017 Frequencies					
Categories	Before	Enter	Exit	Exit x opa	Remain
C1	45	7	3	2	47
C2	10	2	2		10
C3	49	4	6		47
C4	21	3	2	1	21
C5	45	0	0		45
	170	16	13	3	170

Calculating the respective relative frequencies is:

(2013-2017) Probability					
Categories (Ci)	Before P(Q)	Get in	Exit P(E)	Exit x opa	Be P(Ci)
C1	0,26	0,04	0,02	0,01	0,28
C2	0,06	0,01	0,01	0,00	0,06
C3	0,29	0,02	0,04	0,00	0,28
C4	0,12	0,02	0,01	0,01	0,12
C5	0,26	0,00	0,00	0,00	0,26
	1,00	0,09	0,08	0,02	1,00

Where
- P (Q): Previous probability
- P (E): Probability of exit for performance
- P (Ci): Probability that the company is of Category *i* of the matrix Council - Property at the beginning of the period

Specifically, the table shows that in the 2013-2017 period (1st Semester):
- $P(C1 \cap E) = 0,02$ (probability of C1 and exit of IBEX-35)
- $P(C2 \cap E) = 0,01$ (probability of C2 and exit of IBEX-35)
- $P(C3 \cap E) = 0,04$ (probability of C3 and exit of IBEX-35)
- $P(C4 \cap E) = 0,01$ (probability of C4 and exit of IBEX-35)
- $P(C5 \cap E) = 0,00$ (probability of C5 and exit of IBEX-35)

The following illustration shows in the Venn diagram the intersection of the *BE* (one category) and *EXIT (IBEX-35) or both events*.

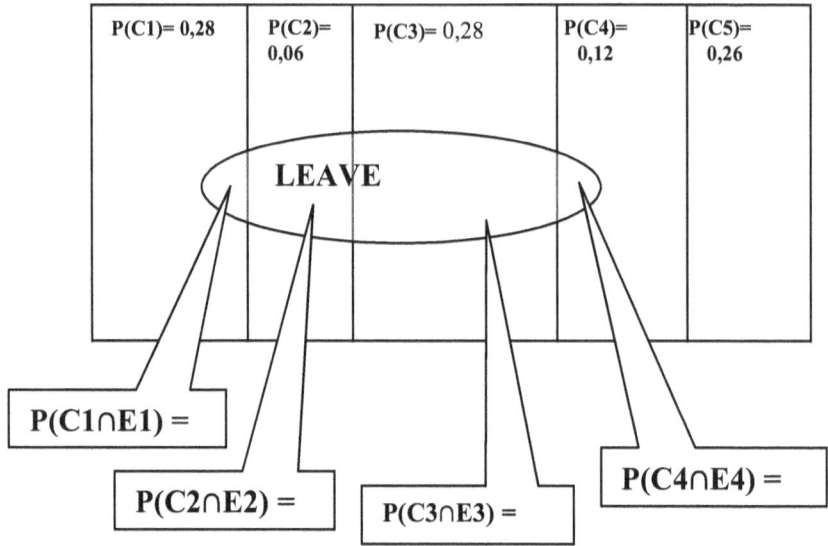

Joint probability P (Ci) and P (E)
Source : Own elaboration

3.3.4.2   Conditional probability of exit belonging to a category

Now, suppose the company belongs to 1 a Category C3, what is the probability that comes out of the IBEX-35?

C3 = Category of the company
E = The company exit the IBEX-35 being C3

It is posed as: we want to know the probability of S if C3 is what is called conditional probability, it is expressed mathematically as:

$$P(E \backslash Ci) = \frac{P(E \cap Ci)}{P(Ci)}$$

Category (i)	2013 – 2017 Probability		
	Be Category i P(Ci)	Joint Ci y Ei P(C Ei)	Condicional - Exit being from Ci -
1	0,28	0,02	0,07
2	0,06	0,01	0,17
3	0,28	0,04	0,14
4	0,12	0,01	0,08
5	0,26	0,00	0,00
Total	1,00	0,08	0,08

Probability Table

We can also see it in the following way:

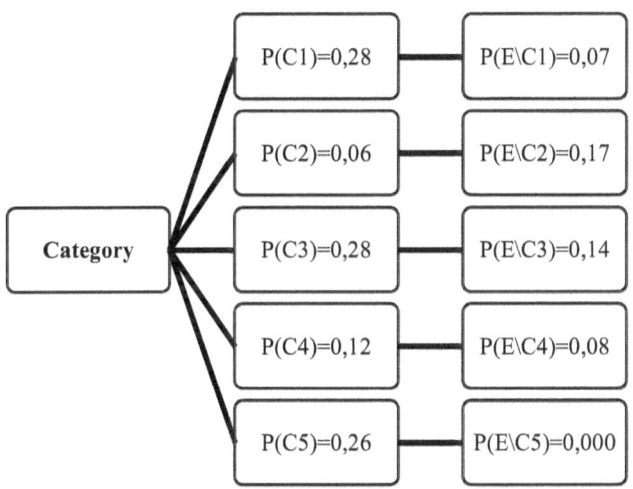

Specifically, the table shows that in the period 2013-2017, the probability of a company leaving the IBEX-35 due to poor performance is:

45

- 0.07 if it belongs to C1
- 0.17 if it belongs to C2 ← **Maximum probability of exit the IBEX-35**
- 0.14 if it belongs to C3
- 0.08 if it belongs to C4
- 0.00 if it belongs to C5

This confirms that the category with the highest probability of exit is C2

3.3.5 Specific objective "B".

Estimate the contribution of the variable THEORETICAL ETHICAL CATEGORY (morphological configuration) to the probability of leaving the IBEX-35.

3.3.5.1 Analysis of automatic detection of interactions (AID)

To perform this analysis we used the statistical technique known as AID, acronym for Automatic Interaction Detection (Automatic Detection of Interactions) that, in addition to studying the dependency relationship between a dependent variable and independent or explanatory multiples, detects the effect and the existing interactions between the explanatory variables, such as his name indicates. It does not provide a function with coefficients that determine the relationship between the dependent variable and the independent variables, but it can be used to complete the analysis and estimate a functional relationship. The main application of the AID analysis is in market segmentation. The independent or explanatory variables used in the AID analysis must be measured with nominal or ordinal scales, and the dependent or explaining variable must be measured with a metric scale (proportional or interval) or dichotomous (values 1 or 0). The AID is based on an analysis of the variance of the differences between the means of all possible dichotomous groups (Santesmases Mestre M., 2011, page 347). With the percentage data of independent directors and the percentage of floating capital, an interdependency analysis (AID) will be carried out, with the objective of validating the segmentation of the proportion of "independent directors - concentration of the floating capital" of the company.

> The Automatic Detection of Interactions (AID) confirms the contribution of 0,766 or almost 77 percent of the variable CATEGORY to the explanation of the variance of the variable PROBABILIDAD DE SALIR of the IBEX-35. This represents a very high variance explanation.

The following is the analysis performed by the DYANE Software (Santesmases) Mestre):

AID ANALYSIS (Automatic Interaction Detection)
==
==

VARIABLE TO EXPLAIN: PROBSAL - Probability of Exit
EXPLANATORY VARIABLE 1: CATEGORY
MINIMUM SIZE OF SEGMENTS: 2
MINIMUM CONTRIBUTION OF THE PARTITION TO THE EXPLANATION OF THE VARIANCE: 1.0%

SEGMENTS PROFILE
==

GROUP 1 : Size: 37; Mean: 0.0185; Desv . standard : 0.0125

GROUP 4: Size: 3; Mean: 0.0360; Desv . standard : 0.0000
- ***CATEGORY: C2 (CONCENTRADO-FUERTE)***

GROUP 5: Size: 13; Average: 0.0300; Desv . standard : 0.0000
- CATEGORY A : C3 (dispersed-weak)

GROUP 6: Size: 12; Mean: 0.0157; Desv . standard : 0.0000
- CATEGORY A : C4 (dispersed-strong) and C1 (concentrated-weak)

GROUP 7: Size: 9; Average: 0.0000; Desv . standard : 0.0000
- CATEGORY A : C5 (dispersed-strong and autonomous)

3.3.5.2 Interpretation

The 76.6 percent of the probability of exit is explained by the category resulting from the "council - property" matrix. The lower average for the case of category C5 (dispersed capital - strong and autonomous board of directors) (GROUP 7). The highest probability of leaving is found in companies of category C2 (concentrated capital - strong council) (GROUP 4), as can be seen in the following illustration.

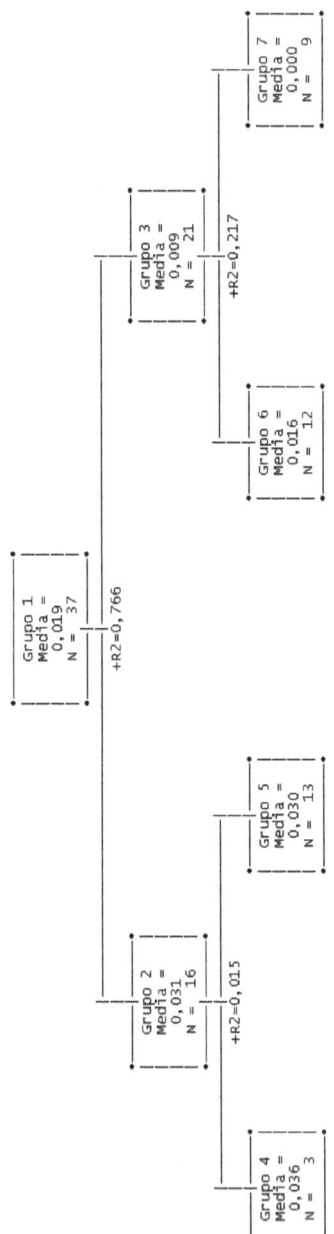

AID Probability of leaving the IBEX-35 by category Board of Directors - Property
Source: own elaboration, software Dyane 2.0 Santesmases Mestre

3.3.6 Specific objective "C"

Calculate a probable average loss value per exit of the IBEX-35 for the morphological configuration.

3.3.6.1 Average loss in quotation when leaving the IBEX-35

The percentage losses in the days prior to the exits of the IBEX-35 (See ANNEX 1) were added to the table "Exits of the IBEX-35", resulting in:

EMP.	MATRIX					YEAR	LOST %
	C1	C2	C3	C4	C5		
GAM				X		2013	8.93
BKIA		X				2013	40.15
ABG			X			2013	15.3
ACX			X			2013	9.29
ELE	X					2013	7.44
EBRO	X					2014	4.26
VIS				X		2014	6.14
ANA		X				2015	5.29
BME			X			2015	8.59
ABG			X			2015	63.24
OHL	X					2016	21.59
S C YR			X			2016	15.72
POP			X			2017	48.02
TOTAL	3	2	6	2	0		

3.3.6.2 Analysis of automatic detection of interactions (AID)

The following is the analysis performed by the DYANE Software (Santesmases) Mestre):

AID ANALYSIS (Automatic Interaction Detection)
================== ==============================
===

VARIABLE TO EXPLAIN: LOST
EXPLANATORY VARIABLE 1: CATEGORIES - (free)
MINIMUM SIZE OF SEGMENTS: 2
MINIMUM CONTRIBUTION OF THE PARTITION TO THE EXPLANATION OF THE VARIANCE: 1.0%
TOTAL PROPORTION OF VARIANCE EXPLAINED: R^2 = 0.1846
SEGMENTS PROFILE
===

GROUP 1: Size: 13; Average: 19.5354; Desv . Est . : 18,1498
Total sample

GROUP 2: Size: 8; Average: 25.7000; Desv . Est. 412,8257
- CATEG: C3 and C2

GROUP 3: Size: 5; Average: 9.6720; Desv . Est . : 37,8672
- CATEG: C1 and C4

3.3.6.3 Interpretation

It can be seen in the illustration that the TOTAL AMOUNT OF LOSS IN THE QUOTATION the days before the departure of the IBEX-35 is around 19%. Being for category C3 and C2 the loss close to 26% (GROUP 2), while for C1 and C4 the loss is lower close to 10% (GROUP 3). For C5 (companies with majorities of independent and independent directors of other ties with the IBEX-35) no aliases have been registered from 2013 to 2017. The AID confirms that 18.46 percent of the variance in the loss per exit of the IBEX-35 is explained with the category resulting from the "director of boar - property " matrix .

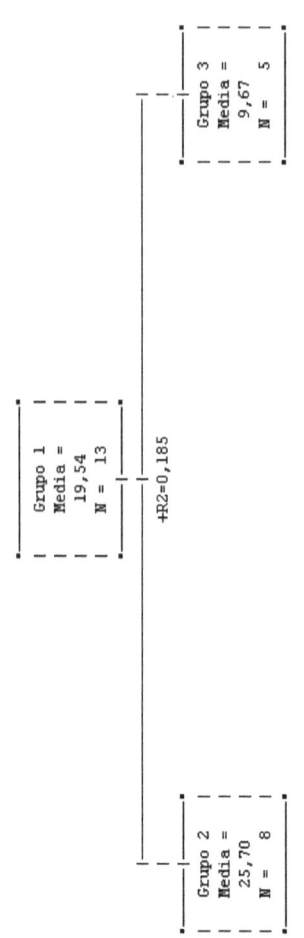

AID LOSS mean segmented by CATEGORY (matrix council - property)
Source: own elaboration, software Dyane 2.0 Santesmases Mestre

3.3.7 Overall objective.

Determine if specific morphogenesis of the board of directors preceded the deep crises that most affected the minority shareholders in the companies that were exit the IBEX-35.

3.3.7.1 CASE ANALYSIS

3.3.7.1.1 BANKIA

Analyzing the morphogenesis of its board of directors as of December 2011 the total number of directors 18, of which: 3 Executives, 6 Proprietary, 5 Independent and 4 Other External. As of May 2012, they cease in their entirety, among them Don Rodrigo de Rato Figaredo - President on 05-09-2012. Entering by cooptation the 10 directors that would close the 1st stage of belonging to the IBEX-35 of Bankia on 12-27-2012, almost 6 months later. The confirmation of that council is of 2 executives and 8 independent ones. Observe how it moves strikingly from Category C1 to C2 in an exaggerated or overactive movement, evidencing a deep crisis, with the consequences for small investors unfortunately already known to all. It is noteworthy that the Category correction occurs in just one month, during May 2012, only 7 months before the brutal exit of the IBEX-35. The movement in the Council-Property Matrix can be seen below:

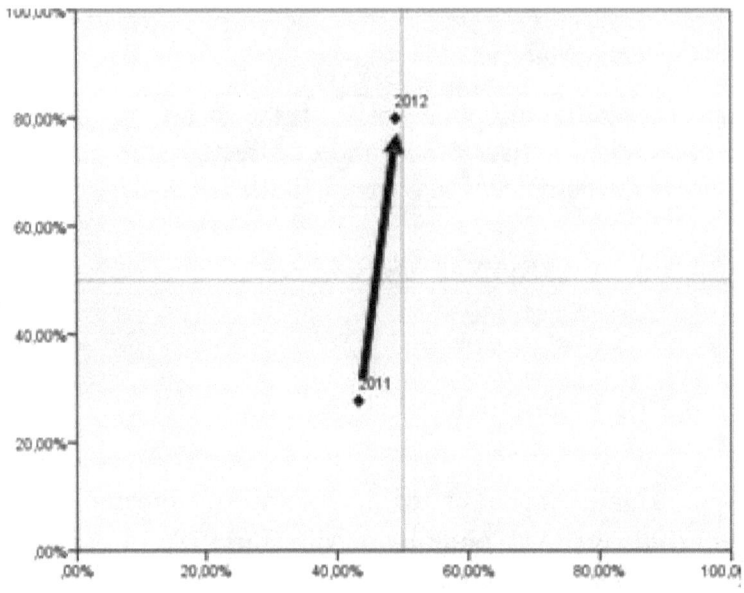

An abrupt change from C1 to C2.
Source: *Own elaboration. IAGC data. IBM SPSS Software*

Conclusions: The Bankia case, the hypothesis that "The exits of the IBEX-35 due to deep crises were preceded by an atypical change in the proportion of independent directors, over and above the usual proportional representation of the free float" is fulfilled.

3.3.7.1.2 ABENGOA

An anomalous sudden oblique movement from C3 to C2 occurs in the 2016 period. This change in the category was accompanied by a loss of close to 50% in the share price when it left the IBEX-35 in November 2015. The evolution of the events is incredibly coincident with the Bankia case at the end of 2012 concerning which it is positioned in the C2 quadrant, but unlike Bankia, Abengoa it does so after the exit of the IBEX-35.

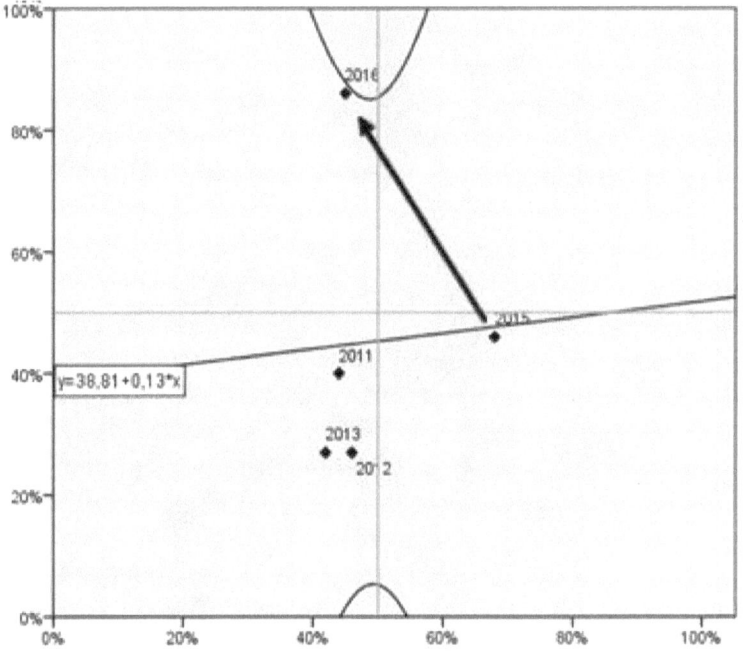

An abrupt change from C3 to C2.
Source : Own elaboration. IAGC data. IBM SPSS Software

Conclusions: The Abengoa case, the hypothesis is not true that "The outputs of the IBEX-35 deep crises were preceded by an unusual change in the proportion of independent directors, above the usual proportional representation of floating capital", and that this one - the increase of representation - took place in Abengoa after the crisis that motivated its exit.

3.3.7.1.3 POPULAR

Atypical change to the independent structure of C3 with direction to C4 in 2016. Prelude of what was to come. Note that the proportion of independent directors falls outside the upper limit of the 95% confidence interval. IBM SPSS software.

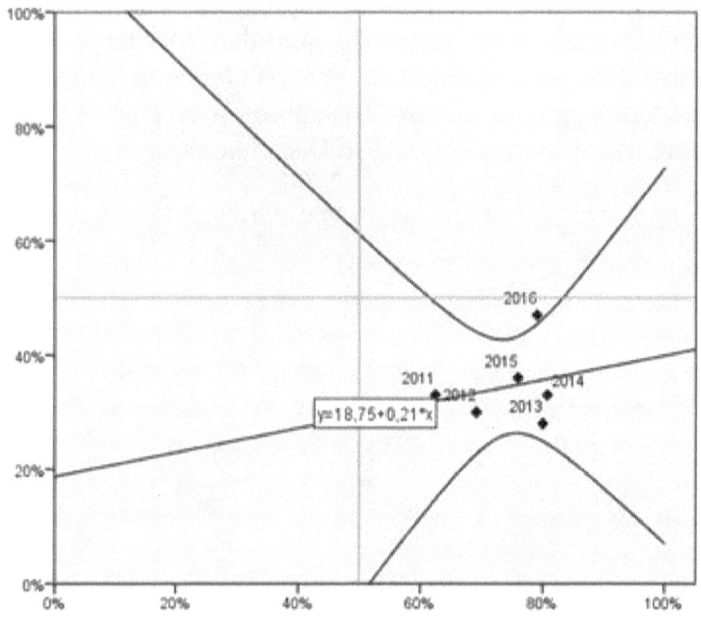

An abrupt change from C3 to C4.
Source : Own elaboration. IAGC data. IBM SPSS Software

Conclusions: The Popular case, if the hypothesis that "The outputs of the IBEX-35 deep crises were preceded by an unusual change in the proportion of independent directors, above the usual proportional representation of floating capital" is fulfilled. Observe how the point cloud is aligned on the trend line except in 2016 when, the proportion of independent directors leaves the upper limit of the confidence interval.

3.3.7.1.4 INTERNATIONAL FOOD DISTRIBUTION - DIA

After the crisis in its board of directors - shown in a series of profound changes, which led to the resignation of its Chairman, and significant changes in its floating capital, the company approached an area of a high risk of exit " C2 "and therefore large losses for its minority shareholders. Indeed, the events were unleashed in an accelerated manner as of July 2018, going from a price of 2.71 euros per share to a minimum of 0.33 to December 11.

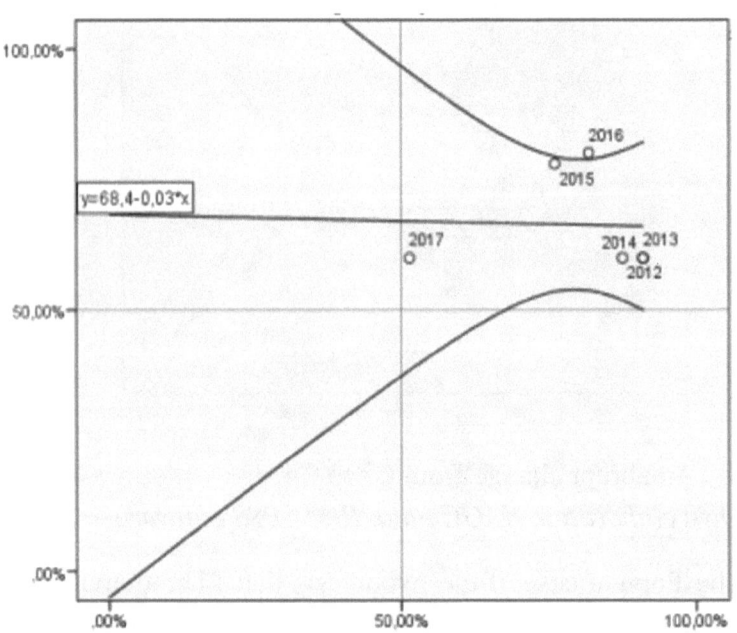

Abrupt change from C4 to C2 .
Source : Own elaboration. IAGC data. IBM SPSS Software

It can be seen in the matrix that at the end of 2017 there is a sudden movement that leaves the board on the edge of C2, coinciding with the higher probability of leaving the IBEX-35 as analyzed in the Conditional Probability of Exiting IBEX-35 belonging to a category.

Conclusions: E n the event day, if the hypothesis that "The outputs of the IBEX-35 deep crises were preceded by an unusual change in the proportion of independent directors, above the usual proportional representation of floating capital" is fulfilled.

Chapter 4

4 CONCLUSIONS AND PROPOSAL

4.1 CONCLUSIONS

According to the results of the investigation, all the objectives could be reached and the hypothesis proposed could be tested.

Research shows that analyze the morphogenesis of the microstructure of the board allows, with amazing accuracy, detect tar early, CAPTURE anomalous ents or atypical variations in the percentages of independent representation of floating capital, Most likely, they will have serious repercussions in the future.

It was confirmed with the technique of Automatic Detection of Interactions (AID), the contribution of 0,766 or almost 77 percent of the variable THEORETICAL ETHICAL CATEGORY to the explanation of the variance of the variable PROBABILITY OF

EXITING of the IBEX-35. This places this variable among the most interesting of analysis for predictive models.

The investigation revealed that there is a high probability of exit by category 2 of the matrix "board of directors - property" and, that the losses the days before departure, when the movement is in the direction of that category, are around 25%. This was confirmed in the cases Bankia, Popular and DIA, where the hypothesis was fulfilled that: "The exits of the IBEX-35 due to deep crises were preceded by an atypical change in the proportion of independent directors, above the usual proportional representation. of the floating capital ".

The investigation also revealed that another theoretical ethical category with high probabilities of exit is C3. Surprisingly, an atypical movement to increase independent representation was registered by Popular months before its exit from the IBEX-35 from that category.

A special mention deserves Abengoa, that, although there was a significant change in its independent proportion concerning floating capital, this occurred after the exit happened. This fact is central because it speaks of discourse full of moral expectations - a large number of independent advisors that are far above normal - but, with the aim, presumably more probable, of recovering from the crisis that generated their exit.

As a complement to the research, it is worth mentioning that the model has been successfully tested in a prediction made in July 2018, in which the abrupt morphological anomaly occurred almost a year before its effective exit from the IBEX-35 occurred. It could be seen that the accuracy of the method of studying the morphogenesis of the microstructure of the Administration Council proved to be amazing.

4.2 PROPOSAL

I understand that the Code of Ethics of the Boards of Directors of 1998 - also known as the Olivencia Code - is up to date. In this respect, on the figure of the independent director, in section 2.1 it is clarified: its primary mission is to enforce the interests of the floating capital in the Board of Directors. As shown in this research, an abrupt change towards an excessively disproportionate representation with floating capital does not mean a greater concern for floating capital, but on the contrary, it must be interpreted seriously as a very likely sign of a crisis with a strong impact. future. In the opinion of the author, should be included in the code of Good Governance of current Listed Companies, a clarification that -in the case of atypical variations that result in exaggerated percentages of representation with respect to floating capital-, explain the reasons that justify said anomalous behavior This would make it possible to discard any doubt regarding the real reasons why such a valuable resource is used for shareholders and, especially, that the discourse that transmits to the different stakeholders - loaded heavily with moral expectations - is used solely for ethical purposes .

BIBLIOGRAPHY

Aldama, E. (8 de 1 de 2003). *Informe de la Comisión Especial para el Fomento de la Transparencia y Seguridad en los Mercados y en las Sociedades Cotizadas*. Recuperado el 28 de 12 de 2014, de https://www.cnmv.es: https://www.cnmv.es/DocPortal/Publicaciones/CodigoGov/INFORMEFINAL.PDF

CEPAL. (2017). *https://repositorio.cepal.org*. Obtenido de https://repositorio.cepal.org: https://repositorio.cepal.org/bitstream/handle/11362/41739/1/S1700425_es.pdf

CEPAL. (2018). *repositorio.cepal.org*. Obtenido de repositorio.cepal.org: https://repositorio.cepal.org/bitstream/handle/11362/43689/13/S1800684_es.pdf

CNMV. (2015). *Código de buen gobierno de las sociedades cotizadas*. Madrid: CNMV.

Código Unificado Refundido, C. (2013). *Comisión Nacional del Mercado de Valores*. Recuperado el 20 de 12 de 2014, de https://www.cnmv.es: https://www.cnmv.es/DocPortal/Publicaciones/CodigoGov/CUBGrefundido_JUNIO2013.pdf

Comisión Nacional del Mercado de Valores. (16 de Julio de 2015). *CMNV*. Recuperado el 16 de 07 de 2015, de Las preguntas que debe hacerse todo accionista : http://www.cnmv.es/DocPortal/Publicaciones/Guias/guia_accionistacc.pdf

ElPaís. (18 de 5 de 2018). *El País Economía*. Obtenido de https://cincodias.elpais.com: https://cincodias.elpais.com/cincodias/2018/05/09/companias/1525871297_046935.html

Fraile, I., & Fradejas, N. (Mayo-Junio de 2010). Heterogeneidad en los Consejos de Administración en España. *Tribuna de Economía IECE*(854), 85-103.

LSA. (2011). *Ley de Sociedades Comerciales - Sociedades Anónimas - Ministerio de Justicia - Gobierno de España*. Recuperado el 29 de 12 de 2014, de http://www.mjusticia.gob.es/: http://www.mjusticia.gob.es/cs/Satellite/1292347054696?blobheader=..QjCNEAZo3cXVnD3gbbhkfEerft1CnRdw

Mace, M. L. (1975). *El Directorio Eficiente*. Buenos Aires: El Ateneo.

Olivencia, M. (1999). *El Gobierno de las Sociedades Cotizadas*. Recuperado el 23 de 12 de 2014, de CNMV: https://www.cnmv.es/DocPortal/Publicaciones/CodigoGov/govsocot.pdf

Stein, & Plaza. (2011). *El papel del consejero independiente en la supervisión y rotación del CEO, estudio 133*. IESE Business Scholl - Universidad de Navarra.

Villanueva, C. U. (15 de Abril de 2015). *Fernando Diéz Stella - Profesor de Derecho Mercantil*. Recuperado el 10 de 08 de 2014, de http://www.fernandodiezestella.com/: http://www.fernandodiezestella.com/derecho_mercantil_1/tema_19.pdf

ANNEXED

Losses the days before the departure of the IBEX-35

Charts quotes days before departure 2012

From the 27th- 12th date on which the news of its exit from the IBEX-35 to the 31/12 becomes public, its price falls 33.5% , while the IBEX-35 falls are on average in that period of 1 , 37% . Next, the table with the opening, maximum, minimum and closing quotes for Bankia is shown . Figure 53 shows the abrupt fall on the day of the public announcement of the departure of the IBEX-35.

Date	Open	High	Low	Close	Volume
Dec 31, 2012	1.64	1.76	1.56	1.56	4,661,886
Dec 28, 2012	1.77	1.80	1.45	1.62	10,300,452
Dec 27, 2012	2.40	2.48	2.20	2.21	5,936,338
Dec 24, 2012	2.76	2.78	2.72	2.74	653,900

The graph shows the impact of the exit of the IBEX-35:

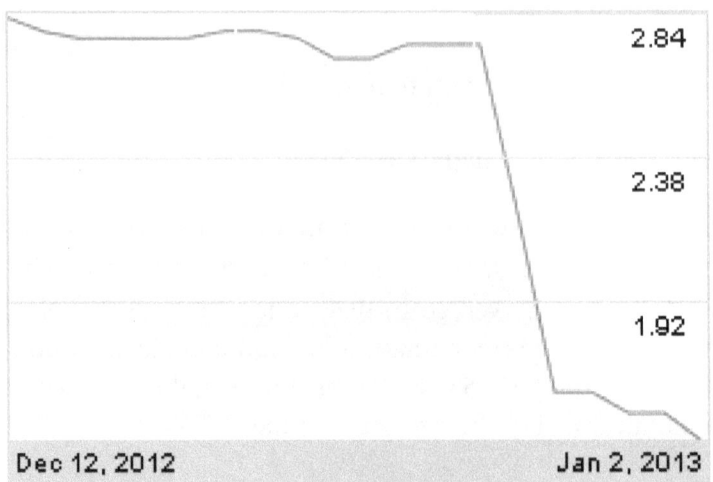

BKIA illustration
Google Finance Source

Charts quotes days before the departure year 2013

Note the Bankia case on December 28, 2012, the share loses 1.08 €
which represents 40.15% of its quotation, just the day after its exit
from the IBEX-35 is publicly announced.

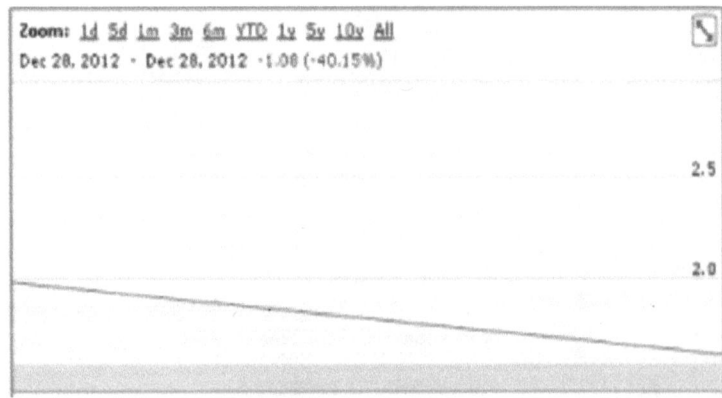

BKIA illustration
Google Finance Source

In the case of Gamesa, the loss was close to 9%.

GAM illustration
Google Finance Source

During the month of June 2013, in twenty days Abengoa loses more than 15% of its value. His departure is made public on July 1, 2013. It is a preview of what would happen almost two years later in 2015 with his second exit but in that case with a loss of more than 60%.

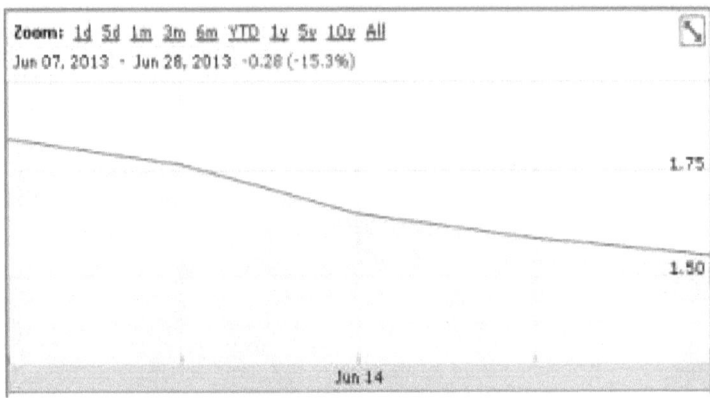

Illustration ABG
Google Finance Source

A week before its departure Acerinox loses more than 9%.

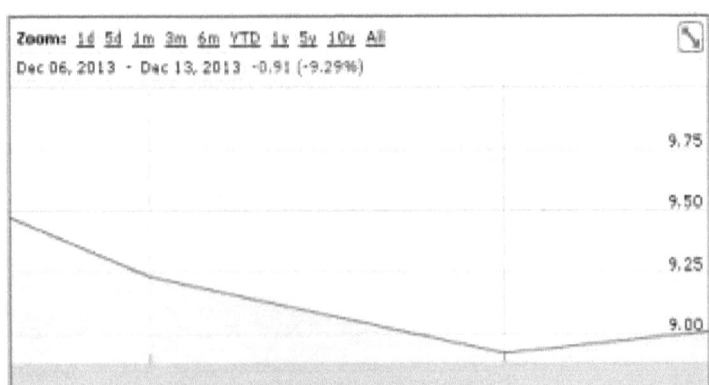

ACX illustration
Google Finance Source

Two weeks before its departure, Endesa loses more than 7% of its market value.

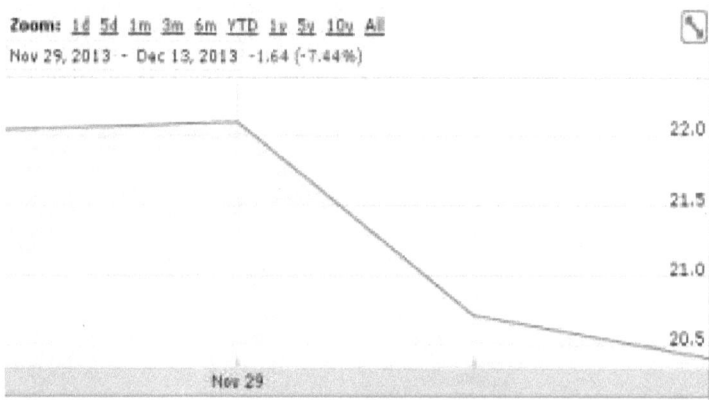

ELE illustration
Google Finance Source

Graphics quotes days before the departure year 2014

Two weeks before departure Ebro Foods loses more than 4%.

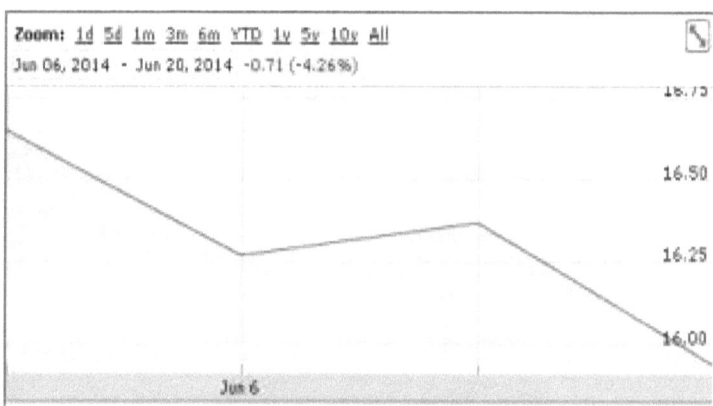

EBRO Illustration
Google Finance Source

Although the official exit of the Viscofan takes place on December 22, ten days before it supports a fall of more than 6% in its market value.

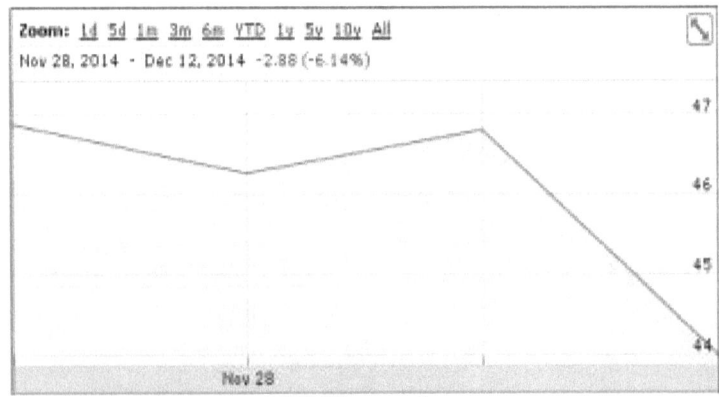

VIS illustration
Google Finance Source

Graphical quotes days before the departure year 2015

Fifteen days before the announcement of his departure Acciona loses just over 5%.

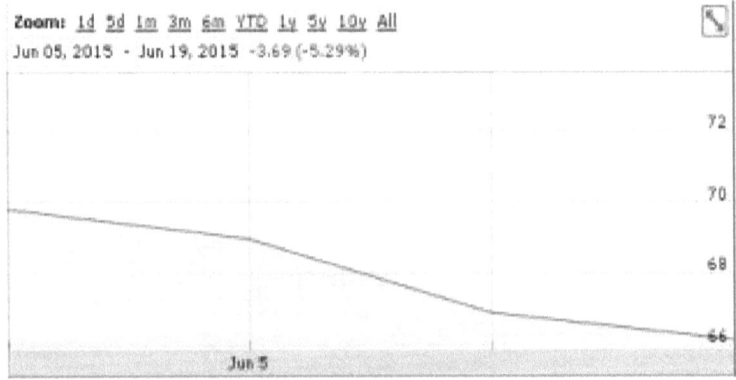

ANA illustration
Google Finance Source

BME loses close to 9% in twenty days before the public announcement of its exit from the IBEX-35.

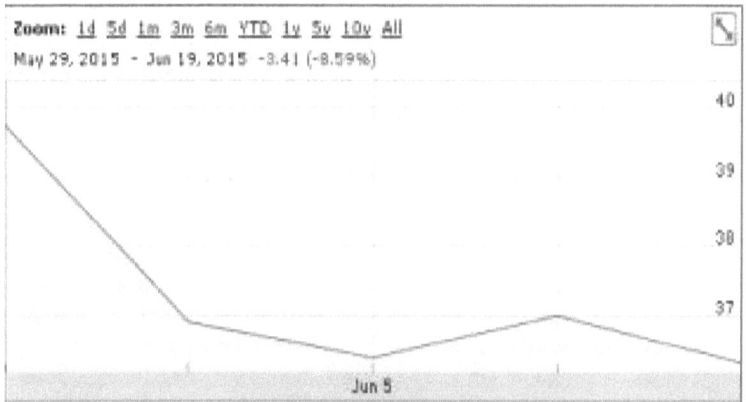

BME illustration
Google Finance Source

Only one week after the announcement of his departure Abengoa loses a resounding 63%.

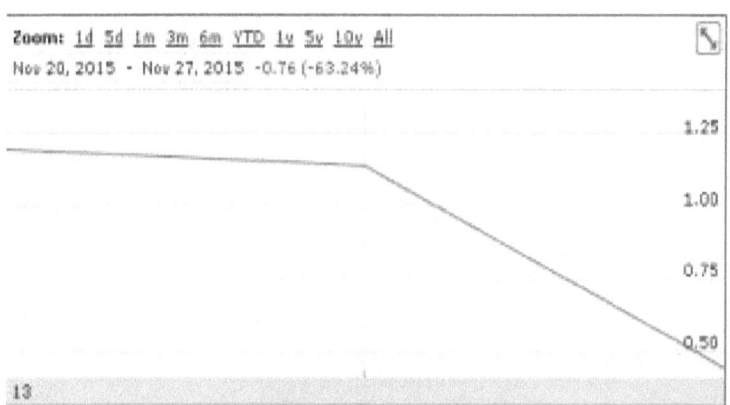

Illustration ABG
Google Finance Source

Charts quotes days before departure 2016

Two weeks prior to the release of OHL, it loses more than 21% of its market value.

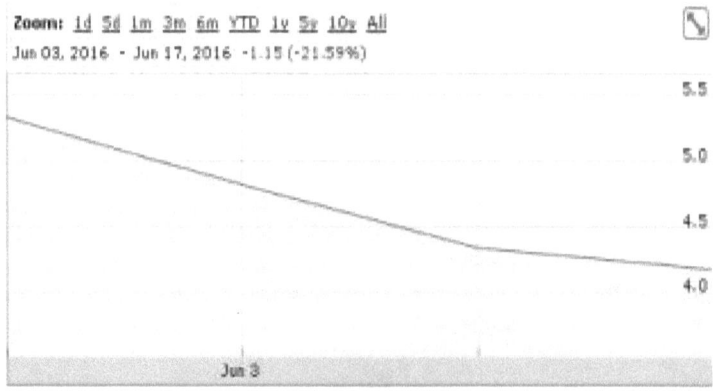

Illustration OHL
Google Finance Source

In the same period as OHL two weeks before the exit of the IBEX-35, Sacyr suffers a loss in market value of almost 18%.

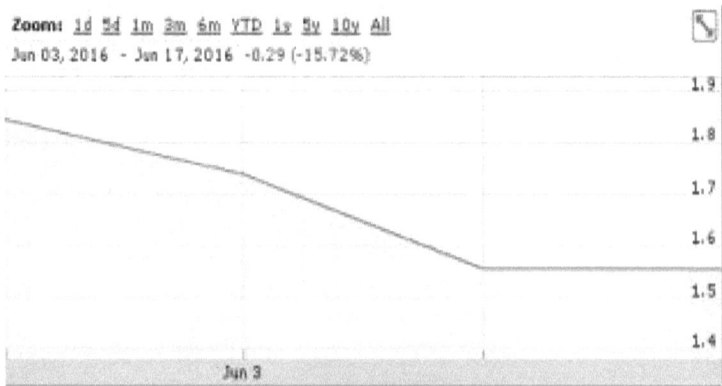

SCYR illustration
Google Finance Source

Charts quotes days before departure 2017

Ten days before the exit Banco Popular Español loses almost 50% of its market value.

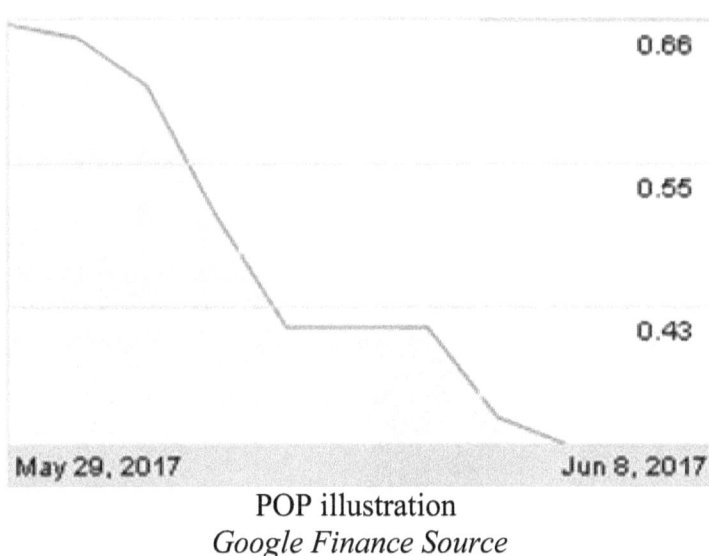

POP illustration
Google Finance Source

www.ingramcontent.com/pod-product-compliance
Lightning Source LLC
Chambersburg PA
CBHW030728180526

45157CB00008BA/3085